LIFE IN THE
RAIN FORESTS

Author: **Lucy Baker**

Consultant: Roger Hammond,
Director of Living Earth

MINNETONKA, MINNESOTA

Copyright © 2000 Two-Can Publishing

Two-Can Publishing
11571 K-Tel Drive
Minnetonka, MN 55343
www.two-canpublishing.com.

ISBN 1-58728-558-4 (hardcover)
ISBN 1-58728-573-8 (softcover)

7 8 08 07 06 05 04

Printed in China

Photographic credits:
p.5 Bruce Coleman p.7 (top) Heather Angel/Biofotos (bottom) South American Pictures/Tony Morrison p.8 Bruce Coleman/E. & P. Bauer p.9 Ardea/Pat
Morris p.10 (top) Ardea/Anthony & Elizabeth Bomford (bottom) Bruce Coleman/J. Mackinnon p.11 (top) NHPA/L.H. Newman (center) Survival
Anglia/Claude Steelman (right) NHPA/Jany Sauvanet p.12 (bottom) Ardea (top) Bruce Coleman p.13 Bruce Coleman p.14 The Hutchison Library/J. Von
Puttkamer p.15 (top) Survival International/Steve Cox (bottom) The Hutchison Library/J. Von Puttkamer p.16 Bruce Coleman/Michael Fogden p.17 Survival
International/Victor Englebert p.18 Impact Photos p.19 The Hutchison Library p.20-21 NHPA p.22 Front cover: Michael & Patricia Fogden Back cover: Tony
Stone Worldwide

Illustrations by Francis Mosley. Story illustrated by Valerie McBride.

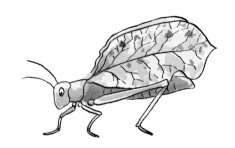

CONTENTS

LOOKING AT RAIN FORESTS

Imagine a forest unchanged for 60 million years, where giant trees reach up to the sky, their leafy branches blocking out light to the forest floor below. Imagine a place where the temperature hardly changes from day to night, season to season, year to year. A place where rain clouds hang in the air and heavy downpours are common. The rain forest is such a place.

About half the world's species of plants and animals live in rain forests. More species of animals live in rain forests than anywhere else in the world.

Rain forests are home not only to large numbers of animals and plants. People have lived in rain forests for generations.

DID YOU KNOW?

● Rain forests are the wettest areas of land in the world. More than 32 feet (10 meters) of rain may fall during a single year in some places.

● More than half of the world's rain forests have been cut down in the last 50 years and the clearance continues. In the late 1990s, we lost another 183 km² of forest worldwide—an area greater than Washington, DC.

LAYERS OF THE RAIN FOREST

Most rain forest life is found about 120 feet (40 meters) above the ground, in the **canopy**. This is where the branches of the giant trees tangle together to form a lush, green platform.

Underneath the canopy, little can grow in the darkness. Where light does get through the canopy, smaller trees and plants compete for space.

Little grows on the forest floor, but leaves and other debris rain down from the canopy. Plants, insects, and animals change this waste into food.

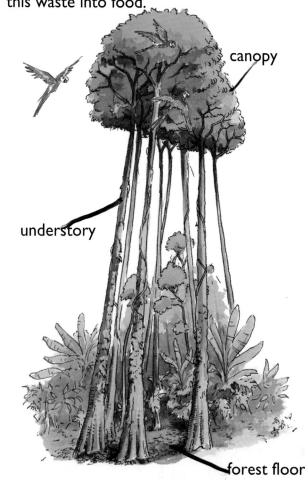

canopy

understory

forest floor

WHERE IN THE WORLD?

More than half of the world's rain forests are in South and Central America. The remainder can be found in parts of Africa, Asia, and Australia. Almost all rain forests lie between two imaginary lines north and south of the **equator**, called the **Tropic of Cancer** and the **Tropic of Capricorn**. This is why they are often called tropical rain forests.

It has been hot and wet in the tropics for millions of years. These constant conditions have made it possible for rain forests to develop into the most diverse and complex **environments** in the world. Some scientists recognize more than 40 different types of rain forest, each with its own variety of plant and animal life.

Rain forests once formed a wide, green belt around the planet, but today pictures taken from space tell a different story. All around the world large areas of rain forest are vanishing as people clear the way for crops, homes, and businesses. Many species of wildlife are disappearing, too.

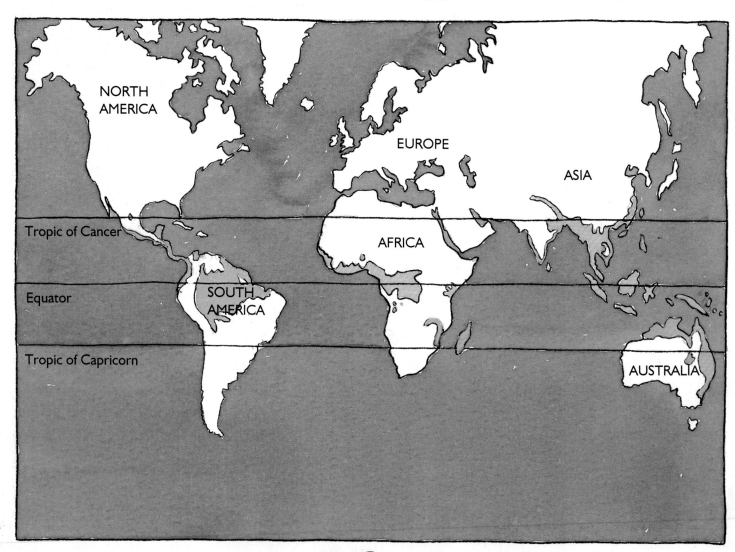

NORTH AMERICA

EUROPE

ASIA

Tropic of Cancer

AFRICA

Equator

SOUTH AMERICA

Tropic of Capricorn

AUSTRALIA

▶ In the tropics, the only change in weather conditions is from wet to wetter during the rainy season. This means that rain forest trees do not need to flower in spring or shed their leaves in autumn. Each type of tree has its own growth cycle. The varying tree cycles guarantee a regular supply of flowers, fruits, nuts, and seeds for rain forest creatures.

▼ The largest rain forest in the world stretches across the Amazon Basin in South America. It covers an area nearly as big as Australia. The Amazon River snakes through the rain forest. It is the largest river system in the world. During the rainy season, parts of the rain forest are flooded by the Amazon and fish swim among the giant tree trunks.

THE PLANT BANK

Most woodlands grow one type of tree such as oak or maple. In the rain forest of South America scientists have counted as many as 280 species in one 2½-acre (1-hectare) area.

Rain forests contain a huge variety of other plants, too. Wherever light reaches the forest floor, an exotic layer of herbs and ferns flourishes. Wiry stems hang like lifeless ropes around the giant tree trunks. These climbers and vines produce a mass of leaves and flowers in the canopy layer.

The canopy itself is like a huge aerial garden. Moss, lichen, and hundreds of flowering plants cover the canopy branches. These plants, called **epiphytes**, do not harm the host tree. Their roots dangle in the air or grow in a thin layer of compost, which forms in the dips and cracks of the many branches.

▲ The rafflesia grows on the forest floor in parts of Asia. It produces flowers up to 3 feet (1 meter) across—the biggest in the world. They have thick, warty petals and spiky centers that stink of rotting meat.

▶ Water and debris collect in some epiphytes and provide ponds for tiny rain forest frogs.

PLANT FACTS

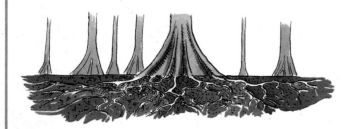

Rain forest trees have shallow root systems, so they often produce special **buttress roots** to help keep themselves standing upright.

Most rain forest leaves are thick and waxy with special **drip-tips** to drain away water. They are often so big they can be used as umbrellas.

FEASTING IN THE FOREST

The lush vegetation of the rain forest is home to millions of different insects and other creepy crawlies. Some, like flies and beetles, act as cleaners, clearing the forest floor of waste and debris. Others, like wasps and bees, help to pollinate the flowers of the forest. Ants and spiders are also in abundance. Between them, they eat large numbers of other insects and so keep them from becoming too plentiful.

The plants and insects of the rain forest provide thousands of different animals with food to eat. Shown here are some of the animals that can be found feasting in the forests.

▲ Lizards can be found all over the rain forest, eating insects, plants, and occasionally, small animals. Most lizards seize insects in their mouths, but a few snatch them from the air with their extra-long tongues.

◄ The giant, red orangutans have huge appetites. They love to eat fruit, but they will also chew leaves, shoots, and tree bark, and occasionally, they will take eggs from birds' nests. To help them find their favorite fruit, the clever orangutans watch the birds that share their tastes in food and follow them through the forest. Orangutans spend most of their lives in the treetops, swinging from branch to branch. Their long, powerful arms and hook-shaped hands make treetop climbing easy work. Orangutans can be found in the rain forests of Borneo and Sumatra in Southeast Asia.

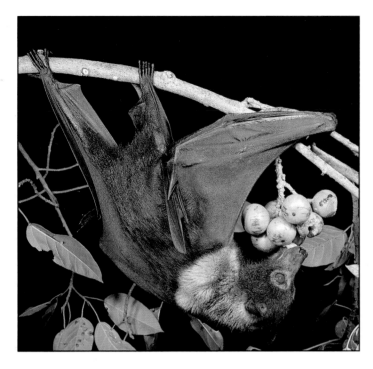

▲ Bats are commonplace in the rain forest. They are not birds but instead the world's only flying mammals. Many bats hunt insects, but some, like the flying fox shown here, eat fruit. Fruit bats help to spread seeds around the forest.

▲ The hummingbird's long, thin bill is ideal for getting to the sweet nectar found inside flowers. But these birds also eat insects. Hummingbirds are flying experts and can even fly backward.

▶ Sloths have strict leaf-eating diets. They spend practically all their time in the treetops. There are two-toed sloths and three-toed sloths, like the one in this picture. Algae, beetles, moths, and mites hide in the sloth's fur.

FOREST FIENDS

The rain forest is a dangerous place. The brightly colored parrots, chattering monkeys, and slumbering sloths may seem carefree, but they have their enemies. When a giant eagle soars overhead or an agile cat is on the prowl, the whole canopy is gripped in terror.

Big cats and eagles are the largest hunters in the forest, but there are hundreds of others. In the canopy, long, slender tree snakes catch lizards, frogs, and small birds. On the forest floor, huge, heavy constrictors, like the anaconda, wait for larger prey such as wild boar or deer that forage in the leaf litter.

Small creatures can pose a greater threat to life. Scorpions, spiders, bees, and wasps are found all over the forest. Many have poisonous bites or stings that can cause rashes, sickness, or even death.

▲ Each rain forest has its own type of giant eagle. In Africa it is the crowned eagle, in South America the harpy eagle, and in Asia the monkey-eating eagle, shown here. Giant eagles catch monkeys, sloths, and other large prey in the canopy layer.

◄ Some forest cats, such as the margay and clouded leopard, are excellent tree climbers. They will chase monkeys and squirrels through the understory. Others, like this jaguar, prefer to wait quietly on low, overhanging branches and pounce on animals as they pass beneath them.

The bushmaster hunts small animals that **scavenge** on the forest floor. It is a venomous snake, which means that it injects poison when it bites. The bushmaster is one of the most feared snakes in South America. Its bite can kill a person within hours. Luckily this snake is shy and not often seen!

PROTECTION FROM PERIL

The smallest rain forest creatures have the greatest number of natural enemies, so it is not surprising that they have developed many ways to defend themselves.

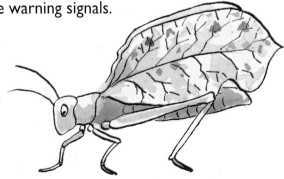

Some rain forest creatures produce a poison in their bodies that makes them unpleasant to eat. Bold markings advertise the fact, and predators learn to recognize these warning signals.

Some butterflies have hidden eyespots on their wings, which are flashed at would-be predators. The false eyes startle the attackers, and this gives the butterflies a chance to escape.

To reduce the risk of being eaten, many insects have clever **camouflage**, like this bush cricket.

RAIN FOREST PEOPLE

Modern people are uncomfortable in the rain forest. They find the hot, humid conditions stifling. Every step they take is fraught with danger, and although there is food all around them, they cannot tell a poisonous berry from a nutritious and refreshing fruit.

Certain groups of people have lived in the rain forests for thousands of years. To them, the rain forest is home and the only world they know. Rain forest **tribes** live in structured communities with their own cultures and customs. They have a deep understanding of the way the rain forest works. They know how to take from the forest without causing harm.

There are rain forest tribes in parts of Africa, Asia, and South America, but their way of life is threatened. Although they have rights according to international laws, they are often mistreated and their land is stolen or invaded. If all the ancient tribes disappear, their detailed knowledge of the rain forest may be lost forever.

▼ A large area of rain forest can support only a few hundred people, so rain forest tribes are spread thinly through the wooded lands. Some tribes build communal houses, where many families live together.

◀ Rain forest children do not have to go to school, but they still have a lot to learn. Their elders must teach them everything there is to know about life in the rain forest.

▼ Many rain forest peoples paint their bodies with colorful dyes and use feathers, flowers, and other natural materials to make simple pieces of jewelry.

PEOPLE FACTS

The Pygmy people of the African rain forest are very small. The tallest Pygmies are only 4 feet 8 inches (1.4 meters) tall.

Life is not easy in the rain forest. A person in the modern world may live for more than 70 years. In the rain forest, few people survive more than 40 years. Diseases like flu and measles, introduced by European settlers, are still big killers of native tribes. More than 80 different tribes have died out in Brazil since 1900.

GIFTS FROM THE FOREST

Rain forest tribes can get everything they need from their homeland. The many different plants and animals found in the forest provide raw materials for meals, houses, clothes, medicines, tools, and cosmetics.

We also use rain forest products. Many of the fruits, nuts, and cereals that fill our supermarket shelves originated in the rain forest. The domestic chicken, which is now farmed worldwide, began its life on the forest floor. The most expensive **hardwoods** such as teak, mahogany, and ebony come from rain forest trees.

Other rain forest products include tea, coffee, cocoa, rubber, and many types of medicine.

We still know very little about the rain forest. Scientists believe there are thousands of future foodstuffs, medicines, and other raw materials waiting there to be discovered.

▼ These tiny rain forest frogs produce a strong poison under their skin to stop other animals from eating them. Some tribes extract this poison by gently roasting the frogs and collecting their sweat. They use it on the tips of their blow-pipe darts when they hunt big game.

RAIN FOREST TREASURES

There is an Amazonian tree that produces a sap very similar to diesel fuel. It can be poured straight into a truck's tank and used as fuel.

One-fourth of all medicines came from rain forest plants and animals.

Rain forest insects could offer an alternative to expensive pesticides. In Florida, three kinds of wasp were successfully introduced to control pests that were damaging the citrus tree crops.

There are at least 1,500 potential new fruits and vegetables growing in the world's rain forests.

▲ A hunter from the Yanomami tribe hunts monkeys and other game, while women and children search the forest floor for food.

RAIN FOREST DESTRUCTION

Rain forests are natural treasure-houses, but they are being destroyed for nothing more than timber and the land on which they stand. This is because most rain forests are found in poor, developing countries. These countries cannot afford to keep their beautiful forests.

Large areas of rain forest are sold to timber companies. They send bulldozers and chainsaw gangs into the forest to cut down the hardwood trees. The wildlife flees and, although only the oldest and largest trees are felled, over half of the forest may be damaged by the time all the work is finished.

▼ An estimated 500 million people have moved into the world's rain forests, and more are sure to follow. They clear the forest to farm small areas of land for food and money.

Rain forests are cleared completely to reach rich mineral reserves, such as iron, copper, or uranium, or to make huge cash-crop plantations of coffee, cocoa, or bananas.

Big business is only half the story. There are thousands of poor, homeless people in rain forest countries who are encouraged to leave the overcrowded cities and farm pieces of rain forest land. They are called **slash-and-burn farmers**, because they build simple homesteads in the forest and then burn the surrounding vegetation to enrich the soil.

DID YOU KNOW?

● Industrial countries buy more than 18 times more hardwood today than they did 50 years ago.

● Over half of Central America's rain forests are gone. They have been cleared to build huge cattle ranches. Much of the meat produced is sold to western countries to feed the demands of their growing burger market.

▶ See the difference between the rich world of the distant green rain forest and the lifeless cracked earth in the foreground? Huge areas of Brazil have been devastated, and animals and plants are gone forever.

PARADISE LOST

It can take less than 10 years for rain forest land to become as barren and lifeless as a desert. This is because most rain forests are found on poor clay soils. Only a thin layer of nutritious **topsoil** covers the forest floor, and this is anchored by giant tree trunks.

Slash-and-burn farmers clear rain forest land to grow their crops. But after only a few years, the tropical rains wash the topsoil away, and the land becomes too difficult to cultivate.

FROM GOOD TO BAD

Trees and plants help to keep the air around us clean. They use sunlight, water, and air to make food. In the food-making process, they make use of the part of the air that we breathe out (carbon dioxide) and produce the part that we breathe in (oxygen).

When rain forests are burned down to clear land, the trees stop using up carbon dioxide. Instead, the forest fires produce carbon dioxide, which pollutes the atmosphere.

The wastelands left behind by farmers are baked by the sun and drenched by rain. The rain, which would have watered thirsty trees and plants, falls straight to the ground and runs downhill, carrying tons of soil with it. Valleys are flooded, and freshwater rivers become clogged with mud.

Tropical scientists believe that, at the present rate of destruction, there will be no rain forests left by the year 2050. If this paradise is lost, thousands of different plants and animals will disappear forever.

SAVING THE FORESTS

More and more people are becoming aware of the need to save the rain forests. Some steps have already been taken to slow the rate of destruction. Native tribes have blocked the path of bulldozers and chainsaw gangs, and many **conservation** groups have launched huge rain forest campaigns.

Much more could still be done to save the world's rain forests. Timber companies could change the way they harvest the forest to reduce the amount of damage they cause. They could also be forced to replant areas of forest that have been disturbed. Slash-and-burn farmers could be taught better ways to farm rain forest lands. By planting trees and crops together, they could preserve the fragile topsoil and use the same piece of land for many years.

Rich, industrial countries could help, too. Rain forest countries are using up their beautiful forests to pay off huge debts to western countries. If these debts were reduced, more money could be spent on developing the cleared land, and the remaining forests could be preserved.

▲ Raoni is a chief of the Kayapo Indians in Brazil. He has traveled many miles (kilometers) from his rain forest home to speak about the problems his people face. Their land has been invaded by foresters and slash-and-burn farmers. The forests, which they rely upon for food and shelter, are being destroyed.

◄ Scientists believe that more than 50 wild species of insects, plants, and animals become **extinct** every day because of rain forest destruction. Many of the world's favorite animals such as tigers and orangutans are endangered because their rain forest homes are being destroyed. By protecting large areas of rain forest, these animals could be saved from extinction.

RAIN FOREST ACTION

Spread the Word
Tell your friends and relatives about the plight of the rain forests. Write to your congresspeople and ask them to help rain forest countries.

Support Rain Forest Campaigns
There are many charities and pressure groups trying to slow the rate of rain forest destruction. They need money and support to continue their work. Watch for news on television, on the radio, or in newspapers and magazines of how you can help them.

THE COWRIE THIEVES

For thousands of years people have told stories about the world around them. Often these stories try to explain something that people do not really understand, like how the world began or where light comes from. This tale is told by the people of the Congo in Africa.

Long ago, in a village right in the middle of the Congo, there lived a man and his wife who were always causing mischief.

All the other villagers agreed that these two had the most irritating habits. They hardly ever did any work, preferring to sit around and chatter to one another. When they did start to work, they would tire of whatever they were doing very quickly and wander off to do something else.

They were always dropping in at their neighbors' huts, just when dinner was ready. Their neighbors were obliged to ask them in to supper; that being the custom.

But the worst thing of all was the way they would pick up other people's belongings. The two of them would just wander into other people's huts and start picking up anything that they could see. They would poke their noses into baskets, take a mouthful of food, or just move everything around so that the owner of the hut would come home to a terrible mess.

The other villagers put up with the pair because they never really did much harm. Whenever a villager lost his temper with them, they looked so hurt at the thought that they had done wrong and promised so fervently to mend their ways. It was impossible to be angry with them for long.

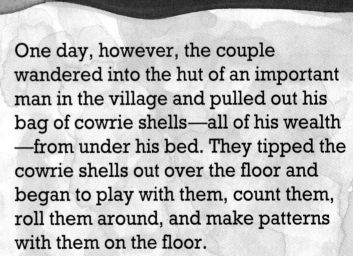

One day, however, the couple wandered into the hut of an important man in the village and pulled out his bag of cowrie shells—all of his wealth —from under his bed. They tipped the cowrie shells out over the floor and began to play with them, count them, roll them around, and make patterns with them on the floor.

Eventually the mischievous man decided to go find some food, and his mischievous wife followed him, leaving the cowrie shells scattered all over the floor.

When the owner of the hut came back and saw his cowrie shells scattered about, his first thought was that he had been robbed.

He shouted to all the other villagers to come and see what had happened. The woman from the hut next door said that she had seen the mischievous man and his mischievous wife coming out of the important man's hut.

Just then, someone spotted the mischievous man and his mischievous wife coming around the corner with a bunch of bananas. They looked very surprised when they were accused of stealing the cowrie shells.

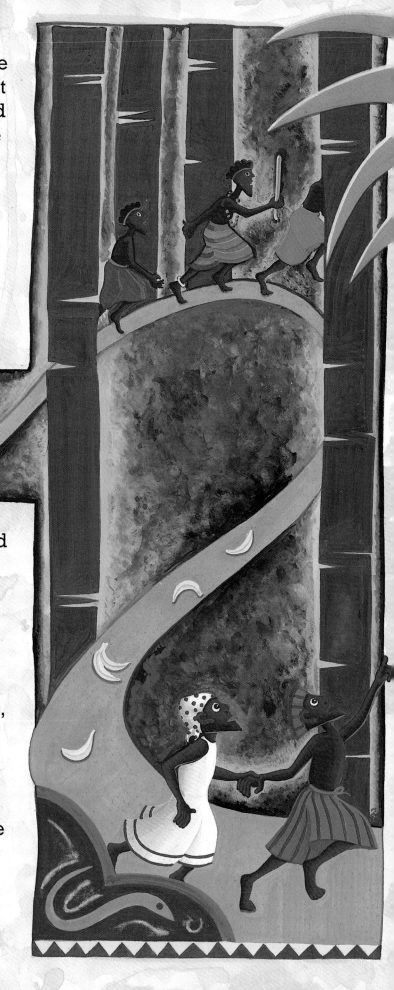

The important man who thought he had been robbed did not wait for an explanation. "Just you wait until I get you!..." he yelled.

He rushed at the pair waving his arms fiercely. The mischievous man and his mischievous wife ran as fast as they could into the shelter of the forest, with all the villagers rushing after them.

When they reached the forest, the mischievous man and his mischievous wife climbed up a tree to hide from the villagers. For a few minutes the villagers chasing them were puzzled. Then one of them spotted the mischievous wife's hair hanging down from a branch.

"Let's sit up here and wait until they go away, and then we will go down," said the mischievous man.

But the villagers didn't go away. The important man who thought that he had been robbed stood at the bottom of the tree and shouted: "Don't think you'll get away with it that easily!"

The villagers set a guard by the bottom of the tree, waiting for the mischievous man and his wife to come down.

Time passed, and the villagers guarding the bottom of the tree changed twice a day, until all of them had guarded the tree once. The mischievous man and his mischievous wife sat in the tree, chattering to one another and pulling off fruit from the nearby branches. Their fingers and toes began to get very long and thin from gripping the branches and stretching out for fruit.

One day, when all the villagers had guarded the bottom of the tree twice, the mischievous man and his mischievous wife realized that the hair on their bodies had grown long and thick, making it hard for them to be seen in the branches.

One day, when all the villagers had guarded the bottom of the tree three times, the mischievous man and his mischievous wife felt a funny sensation at the bottom of their spines. They had grown tails! They jumped up and down on their branch, chattering to one another very fast and swinging with their new tails.

The villager at the bottom of the tree heard all the noise and stared up at the pair. What a surprise he got! The mischievous man and his mischievous wife had turned into monkeys!

When the villager went back to the village to tell the others what he had seen, the important man who thought he had been robbed was furious. But later, when he had counted his cowrie shells, he realized how unjust he had been. How he regretted his hastiness!

And that is why, even though the people of the Congo are often annoyed with mischievous monkeys who come into their houses and make a mess or take their food, they never harm them.

TRUE OR FALSE?

Which of these facts are true and which ones are false? If you have read this book carefully, you will know the answers.

1. Rain forests are found all over Europe.

2. Rain forests lie between the tropics of Capricorn and Cancer.

3. There are up to 40 kinds of rain forests.

4. Orangutans are found in the forests of Africa.

5. As many as 280 tree species have been counted in one $2^1/_2$-acre (1-hectare) area of rain forest.

6. The world's largest rain forest is in Australia.

7. Algae and insects shelter in the long fur of the sloth.

8. Giant eagles feed on animals from the forest floor.

9. Chickens originally came from the rain forest.

10. Tribespeople collect poison from rain forest frogs by squeezing them.

11. Sap from a tree in the Amazon basin can be used as diesel fuel in trucks.

12. Slash-and-burn farming helps the soil to grow richer.

13. The rain forests may be destroyed by the year 2050.

Answers: 1. False 2. True 3. True 4. False 5. True 6. False 7. True 8. False 9. True 10. False 11. True 12. False 13. True

GLOSSARY

● **Buttress roots** develop to support heavy tree trunks and help keep the tall trees of the rain forest upright.

● **Camouflage** is the method by which the surface of certain creatures is covered in patterns or colors that match their backgrounds. These help to hide them from predators. A chameleon can change its body color according to the background it walks against.

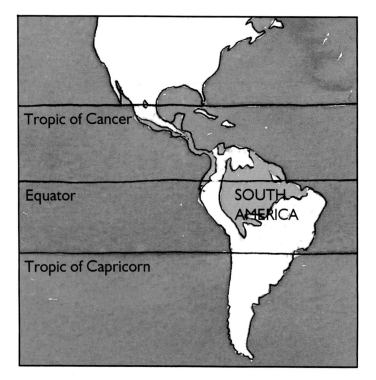

● **Canopy** is the uppermost layer of the rain forest. It is the dense leafy section some 18 to 21 feet (6 to 7 meters) deep and 120 to 150 feet (40 to 50 meters) above ground.

● **Conservation** is the preservation of natural species and environments that have been exploited by humans. It involves help from governments and scientists.

● **Drip-tip** is the long tip on most leaves in the rain forest that sheds rain from the leaf's waxy surface.

● **Environment** is the particular combination of conditions in an area, which affects the type of living things inhabiting it.

● **Epiphyte** is a plant that grows on another plant without damaging it.

● **Equator** is the imaginary line exactly halfway between the North and South poles.

● **Extinct** means that the last member of an animal or plant species has died out as a result of overhunting, a change in its habitat, or its failure to compete with a new animal or plant.

● **Hardwood** trees such as ebony, teak, and mahogany grow in the rain forest. Their tough wood is excellent for making strong furniture, and this is one cause of the destruction of large parts of the rain forest.

● **Scavenge** is to feed on the refuse left by others, for instance, on another animal's kill.

● **Tropic of Cancer** and **Tropic of Capricorn** are imaginary lines at about 23° 27'' north and south of the equator, at the point where the sun changes its course over the earth's surface. The area between these two lines is known as the tropics and most rain forests are found in this region.

● **Understory** is the name for the smaller trees and bushes that make up the middle level in a rain forest, below the tops of the taller trees.

● **Slash-and-burn farming** is practiced by poor farmers who clear areas of the rain forest for soil on which to grow their crops. These farmers move on every few seasons, as the soil holds little good once the trees have gone.

● **Topsoil** lies above the stony ground beneath the rain forest floor. This rich earth is held in place by the trees but is rapidly washed away by rain when the trees are cut down.

● **Tribe** is a community of people who live together for protection from danger and for a shared way of life.

INDEX

RESOURCES

Chameleons on Location, by Kathy Darling, 1997. Fifty-three of the 128 known species of chameleons are found in the endangered rain forests of Madagascar. The author and her photographer daughter traveled to this area where they studied this fascinating lizard.

Interfact Rain Forests, by World Book, 1997. This CD-ROM and book work together to help students learn about rain forests and the animals that live there. The disk is full of interactive activities, puzzles, quizzes, and interesting facts. The book contains fascinating information highlighted with lots of full-color illustrations and photographs.

Journey into Amazonia,
http://www.pbs.org/journeytoamazonia/
A fun, colorful Web site on the disappearing Amazon rain forest for teachers and students, with interactive activities.

Rain Forest Action Network,
http://www.ran.org/ran/
Rain Forest Action Network is an organization dedicated to helping preserve the earth's rain forests. This Web site presents information about rain forests and the Network's campaigns to save them. Includes a "Kids' Corner" section with information about life in the rain forest and what kids can do to save the rain forests.

Rainforest Alliance,
http://www.rainforest-alliance.org/
This international nonprofit conservation organization presents rain forest facts and learning activities for kids and teachers.

Science in the Rain Forest,
http://www.pbs.org/tal/costa_rica/
An electronic field trip presented by PBS.

Tropical Forest Mammals, by Elaine Landau, 1996. This book introduces children ages 5-8 to animals that make their home in tropical rain forests.